Everything I Write
Is a Love Song to the World

Everything I Write
Is a Love Song to the World

poems by
David McIntire

MOON
TIDE PRESS

~2019~

Everything I Write Is a Love Letter to the World

Editor-in-chief
Eric Morago

Associate Editors
José Enrique Medina, Michael Miller

Marketing Specialist
Ellen Webre

Proofreader
Jim Hoggatt

Front cover art
"A Salute from the Underground" drawn by M. Segal with color by 11:21

Book design
Michael Wada

Moon Tide logo design
Abraham Gomez

Everything I Write Is a Love Letter to the World
is published by Moon Tide Press

Moon Tide Press #166
6745 Washington Ave. Whittier, CA 90601
www.moontidepress.com

FIRST EDITION
Printed in the United States of America

ISBN # 978-1-7339493-0-9

for Arm

who once held my face to the light
and watched me smile

Contents

Introduction (A Momentary Indulgence)

Herein, dear reader, you will find songs of love and songs of hunger.

If you survive long enough in this universe, you find that it is the singing that counts most of all. You find that it matters less how you sing and much more that you sing. I have known this and yet had somehow buried it deep within the folds of my losses and fears. I had secreted this knowledge as far too powerful for me to handle. I had denied myself all of the music that flows in my veins, all of the tears that feed me, all of the tiniest sighs reserved for the perfect moments, all of it hidden from my own eyes in an attempt to live correctly.

Herein are the field dressings of love. Herein you will find the repair work and the discovery once again of discovery. Herein you will learn how one man failed himself for years before once again remembering his song, remembering his choreography, remembering finally that he had a voice…one worth using.

Come, dear one, join me in this campfire dance, this bedtime story of frightful cacophonies, this place setting for the memories we no longer need. Come…

Secrets Only the Sky Can Tell You

your mother has wept far more tears
than you will ever count

the trees will wait for you…always…

only the shadows will welcome you
every time you come home…everything else wavers

love you will suffer
love you will wail
love you cannot endure

…endure anyways…

the moments you fear
are not the ones you should

the moments you long for
are not the ones you need

the lifetimes you imagine
cut like hope

in a moment of weakness
you will have a moment of weakness

it will take too long for you to realize
that life is just fragments
randomly glued together
only our translations
attempt to make any sense at all

everyone you know is lost
everyone you know is on fire

only i am allowed to tell you this…
and you will never believe me…

She and He

he left her, she said
with a head and a heart
full of electric fuzz

he missed a turn
on the way home
and took the scenic route
through the darkened streets and hills

she left him, he was sure
with a mystery
a beautiful mystery
and a strange sky
under which he could fold his sorrow
and his aspirations
like napkins at the restaurants he could never afford
she left him with a calm insistence
that clung to him
that lingered in his hair
that fell into his pockets
that gave him drunken affirmations

he left her, she said
with a mouth full of words
she could not quite pronounce
with ears full of excitement
with eyes full of permission

he drove with almost no aim
just taking in the circumstances
within which he was present
within which he sang low and soft

he drove...
falling in love with the darkness
the way he had done once before
falling in love with tomorrow
pretending he knew it would come...

This Nothing

for my no one
not no one
but mine nonetheless
my almost something
my never was

my no one
how i adore you
my mine not mine
my always never was
my intimate stranger

this nothing
is for you
it is all yours
everything i can fit
into this invisible box
as a gift for you
my no one
my mine not mine

this is why you will leave me
this is the way i fail
this time
my mine not mine
my almost never always
i am no one
and you will not take me home
you will not know my secret name

i have already given you my everything
you may as well take my nothing too

Yet to Dance to

freeways form ladders
that climb us up
into a hell of our own construction
we build our homes
with gravestones and broken promises
see us water the roses with our piss
it is the only place
we can lose ourselves

this city
this concrete dirty
this beast that weeps
we love dying slowly here
we dream of her skyline

traffic signals sweep past us
with such speed
it becomes an industrial rainbow
we learn to make up names
for the homeless
we try to sell our imagination on etsy
as hand-picked, organic mystery

we get no offers

this city is an echo in reverse
it is the sorrow of imaginary tragedies
we hug ourselves in the streets of this city
it is the only place
we can find ourselves

find my name
on the side
of what once was a beautiful building
i am climbing this ladder
the same as anyone
but i am climbing to my own soundtrack
i am climbing toward freedom

for it cannot be found in these streets
we are only free to lose
our sense of direction
this
this is the calling card we leave
this is the kiss we dream of
but upon which we cut ourselves
this is the dance we must execute perfectly
under pain of a gravelly chastisement
a formerly married voice over artist
greasing our arrogance and our failures alike

dearest ones,
i am sorry for the days i forgot your names
forgive me for the broken glass
and the tired voice mails
please allow me to impale myself
upon your imaginary retribution

dearest ones,
it is my adoration for your consequences
that holds my attention at attention

dearest ones,
there are songs we have yet to dance to

come
climb with me
let us dance in our own hell
the towers of greed
gleaming in the sunrise
disdain our rhythms

come
this is *our* hell
my hand awaits you
my feet are in love
with your shadow

Cannot

i write the words of your face
i write the words of your breath
i write the words of your curves

but your eyes

i cannot write the words of your eyes
i can only look into them
and try to believe that i am alive

Almost Built

i cannot touch your anger
i cannot drink your tears
you have barred me from your embrace
from your secrets
from your poetry

i cannot dance with your tongue
i may not whirl in the air with your name
you are more than just echoes
but i will stand at the curb
and wave as you fade

i cannot ignore what remains
of the us we almost built
but i will hold it gently
down this walkway of forever

Along the Harbor

stop...
listen to the waves
see the moon
weep for your city
...love her

Her Eyes

her eyes are colored magic
singing iris
echoing lash
melodies of strange

her eyes borrow noisy rhythms
her lungs too full of words
her cheeks full of wonder
every smile rising from the eyes

every smile

a colored magic

every smile

a tired glory

every smile

a warm goodbye

In Love with the Sun

i spend hours a day
thinking about the inconceivable
trying to name the eternal
wondering if time can actually be wasted
dancing in foreign languages

i spend days a week
finding the lost
losing the wonderful
wondering about the infinite
deciding not to go crazy...yet

i spend weeks a year
dying slowly
turning from one sky to another
falling in love with the sun
but only sleeping with the night

i spend years of my life
trying to die well

Song in Search of a Singer

i cannot say it any clearer than this:

she is my leonard cohen
i am her joe strummer

You

you you you
you are not the moon light
not the alley way
you
still, you…
it is your face i see
it is your voice i tremble
it is your skin i wait for

you still you
and the night is not as long
i
gaze drunk at the waves
i
keep to myself at the bar
i
think of you and smile
i
think of you and weep…just a little

you
you
it is your skin i tremble
it is your eyes i long to see
looking at the moon light
looking down the alley way
trembling at the waves

you are not
you are not
you are so not so much
you are
you are so you
you are you
you
i
still
your face

your face
your eyes
you
you
you

To You

i think i have something to say to you
i think that i need to ask forgiveness from the moon
i have not appropriately respected her journey in years

i bow to the night and beg

i think this is part of what i must say to you
i think that i need to hold your hand
and stare softly into those eyes…

…those eyes

i think that i must kneel before you
you and the night
i think that i will find new songs
and new stars to pull down in tribute
new lies to burn with the dawn

i think that i must ask your permission…

…for everything

When it Should

be
here
now
the light is inventing psychedelia once again
here
now
dancing through clouds
glowing when it should sparkle
sparkling when it should shimmer
shimmering when it should wash
over me
here
now

Once Again

Dear One,

your skin
when it touches my lips
is a moment
a long moment
your skin
when it touches me
is *the* moment

your skin
is the moment
that is what i must tell you,
dear one,
for this is a cautionary tale
and must contain a warning
your skin
is a trap
a lure
a blind negotiation full of secrets

understand me, dear one,
i am the willing victim
the permitted experiment
the test that woos the stars

understand me, dear one,
the taste of your skin
the scent of your mystery
the want in your face
all call to me
my mouth longs to say your name
my nose is eager to seek out your imaginations
my arms ache to pull you into a universe
you have never heard of

but your skin
when it caresses my lips

that is a moment
a moment of unintelligible clarity
it is the stars blinking, finally blinking

dear one,
i long to see the stars disappear
once again...

Rationale

when it is time to see you
i arrive with a smile
when it is my turn to go
it is always with hesitation

and a look back

i'm taking these
as good omens
i'm taking these to exchange them
for a simpler currency
one that sings like the starlings
so that i'll know…

…i'll just know…

For that Fall

she is breakable
she is true
she is undeniable
and more than a little yes!

you find yourselves entwined
trying hard not to break
gently falling
even knowing it will end in broken days
softly falling
even knowing the river is dry
immensely falling
right past every red alert

she is breakable
but sings so fearlessly
it almost seems a futile gesture to kiss her gently
but kiss her gently you do
and she you
and the exchange is glorious
and accidental
and sparklingly warm
and so you kiss her more roughly
suddenly remembering
that she is breakable
and then just as suddenly remembering
that it's not that kind of breakable
and so you roll her over and kiss the small of her back
but she is breakable and true
and so you hold back...just slightly
not wanting to risk that break
that fall
that immensity...

...but oh, that fall

you just might give everything
for that fall...

Cross My Heart...

you know that thing you do
when you encompass me?
can you...
can you stop that...please?
that thing you do when you find the off switch
for the stars
when the bats' echolocation becomes
a big band horn arrangement
can you stop that?
can you please draw the shade on our words
and slay me with muffled qualifications?

i promise
that i will attempt
to think of you with decreasing frequency

i will fail

there is nothing we cannot sing
once we bother to learn the melody
i will sing of the unbidden
the unbridled
i will sing of encompassing

i promise
that i will attempt
to sing of you with decreasing frequency

i promise
that i will fail

Have You Looked?

i am lost in you

how is it then possible
that you have not yet found me?

Amazed

where do you go
when you're not with me?
what touches your hands?

i have no secret view
only the sacred desire for your skin
your breath
i cannot see you but in my dream
the only dream i have any more

i watch amazed at your clouds
the stars are gossiping kindly with the shadows
when you move
it is as if the universe turns around you
there are kittens and black holes
and ambient lighting
but none of that matters
because it is your eyes that call me
it is your lips that draw me
and i am again, amazed

but the dream never answers any questions
it never records your hands when they move
when they question the wind
when they brush the back of my head
and all i can do is fall onto your breast
and hold back my tears
just breathe, my love
that is all i require of you
just breathe

And if She Isn't

when we bleed words
as an occupational hazard
when we cut ourselves on stage
in order to feel
when we run from ourselves
into tired bricks
and hollow disguises
we are only echoing our losses
the most intimate of our failures

when we cry out loud
it is not a performance
not even in the spotlight
when we cry silently at night
that is when we are bombastic
and full of our own ragged truths
the ones that make us cry for so long
for the lies are nothing
only truth can hurt us

when we finally surrender to our vulnerabilities
when the pavement shimmers at our footsteps
when the alleyways call us by name
that is when we seek out the hollow places
that is when we are dropped unceremoniously
into the revolving adventure
that is when we kiss
for the first time
and discover that she is the world
she is always the world
and if she isn't
we will make her so
that is our charm
and our harm
it is our moment in the moment…

…for years, it will be the only one we know

Colors

there is a silent empty combat
an exchange
between two men
passing on the street

see me, brother
we are still wild
and must show our colors

Hurt Teaches

Being alive is the hurtingest poetry there is.

— Andy Sykora

this is not a sad song
no lamenting here, dear ones
we are warned inadequately
but hold no grudge
our elders are as susceptible as we

breathe in, dear ones
breathe deep, so deep that it brings pain to your lips
know that this is the magic spell
you cast every day
know that the speed of light
is your ally
know that pain is your friend

yes, dear ones, we weep
yes, we wail
and we are daily falling in amazing and horrifying ways
yes

but, my dear ones, i tell you this in confidence
it is the tears in the sun that prove you
it is the laughter against the night sky that proves you
no lamenting here, my loves
we are simple creatures made complicated by our fears

breathe, dear ones, breathe
i tell you this
it will hurt
it will hurt to breathe
but oh, that hurt teaches us so much

breathe and know
that you are here
know that we are all breathing

I Want to Know

am i allowed to miss you
is it permitted for me to notice the space
where you no longer are?

and in this arm's length romance
how close are you to knowing?
how far are you from all the pitfalls you have labeled?
don't you know by now
pitfalls are by nature invisible
and our tiger trap affair
has us both flailing?

answer me if you don't want to hear from me
ignore me if you love me
buy more hours on your meter
if you want to leave
tell me when you have gone
write to me if i have gone
relate to me the mundane moments of your day
sing to me that you have learned my secret name
that you know my most resilient lullaby
hum the combination to my locker
and all that is still hidden inside
is yours

but you are not singing to me
not that you know of anyway
i hear melodies rising from your skin all the time
but they are meant only for me
someday i will tell them to you
someday we will know the words that go with it
and we may then laugh
and we may then turn darkly away
either way i will sing
please join me in that song
please explain harmony to my head
dispel all the shiniest lies
and tell me please

am i allowed to miss you?
i want to know
that space that isn't you
is getting bigger

As Your Name

the whispers i heard as your name
tumbling from those lashes
from those eyes
cannot compete
with the starlings singing you home
with the blustering butterflies shooing you from my window

(the starlings want what you want
but they are notoriously unwise birds)

go
it's alright
i only heard the whispers
i did not speak them…

…not till you left

Poet's Prayer

oh moonlight
oh sorrow
oh one-legged wonderment
i call on you
oh misinterpretation
oh glory
oh low tide
i sing to you
i call your name
and wonder
oh drunken glory
oh beautiful entanglement
i cry for your subtlety
i cry for your instrument
oh rhythm
oh fallen angel
oh low tide
tell me of your sorrows
tell me that i have missed something
oh loneliness
oh wonderment
if you know me
i will be supple and encouraging
if you need my name i will wail
oh sandy admissions
oh tidal wisdom
oh sorrowful
oh midnight
oh traffic jam
sing in the key of disorder
sing in the key of love
oh misanthrope
oh innocence
i miss you
i call on your love
i call on your song

Sing and Wither

if you fall in love with the shadows
you are lost

if you fall in love with the sky
you are saved

if you fall in love with both
you are lucky
because you travel everything in between
and see how close they really are to each other

it is in the in-between
where you will find sorrow
but only as it connects to joy
you will find uselessness
coupled with ecstatic purpose

it is in the in-between
where love comes to life
where you examine every rusted facet of it
let the tetanus take hold
you can feel your joints slowly cementing
into exultation

if you fall in love with the moon
you shine

if you fall in love with the sun
you sing and wither

if you sing your sorrow
it will leave you and last forever

if you sing your joy
it will decorate you with sparkling intensity

and we will join your dance

When She Walks Away

i read the words she has brought to me
hugging each serif tenderly with my curiosity

i touch the words she brought to my door
tracing the surface in search of the right accent
wondering which of the syllables dropped from her tongue

...there must be at least one...

i read the words she has presented to me
seeking the same answers
to different questions
her pen changing colors in mid-sentence
just to keep things interesting

i read the words she brings
because when she walks away
the words still vibrate with her immediacy

as do i...

as do i...

Wide Open Until I Die

and so shall i continue to confess
my weaknesses to the world?
do i possess no ability to hold my virulent tongue?
am i destined
to expose my heart to every smile?

this is too much
and always has been

am i a masochist?
or full of hope?

either way
i know i will not stop…

It's…

it's when she reaches across the table
to take my hand
it's when she takes almost too long to look away
it's the end of everything
it is the filibuster of raw desire

it is her fingers
climbing into my palm
it is the sorting out of missing intentions
and almost victories
it's the two seconds of amazing
she allows me to see in her eyes
as her hands make my skin pray

it is everything i cannot say
except for one
i know now
she will never stay

It is Here

we are hung between our determination
and our failures
it is no mystery how we got here
we made every decision
and we weep with that knowledge daily
we are slid between the sheets
of paperwork bound to our footsteps
the documentation of our days
the certification of our existence
wobbles behind us
unconcerned with our aspirations
merely barnacled onto our consciousness
the hard shadow of our regrets
we are strung between our melodies
and our dissonance
it is no mystery how poorly we sing
what is never revealed
is that it is not the notes you hit
it's the notes you feel
it's the notes you bleed
it's the notes calloused on your palms
cut into your face
the tracks of every broken word of love
the residues of ecstasy
we are tethered between the attack
and the sustain
and it is here we sing our notes
it is here we breathe

In the End

my fingertips on your skin
my breath, warm on your neck
your head counting my heartbeats
the slow up and down of my chest

i am the mockingbird at your window
it is my cacophony that wakes you
i know no kinder way

perhaps it was the stunning formations
my starling
my nymph
that drew me here
perhaps it was the way your wings spread
when you sang to me of the sky

but my fingertips will not hold you
and my breath will not hold you
and my heartbeats will not hold you
and will now go uncounted

and your song, dearest starling
will become strange and distant
and i will forget where your window is in the end

The Only Song We Know

pour whiskey down my throat
and i may figure out what to say
i might determine just how to reach
across this self-imposed chasm

pour whiskey down my throat
and it may just come to pass
that my words fall out in order
that my synapses will kaleidoscope into rationality
and my syntax erupts into wisdom

pour whiskey down my throat
if you want me to dance with you
it's the only way
and not a pretty way by any measure

pour whiskey down my throat
and beckon to me from across the alley
call my name in concrete canyons
filled with static and despair
we will run half blind with glory and disappointment
fleeing the boredom of our lives
falling into misspent choruses of punk rock anthems

pour whiskey down my throat
and together we will burn the grand façade
we will call down the broken angels
and punish them for telling the truth
by telling them the most beautiful of lies

pour whiskey down my throat
for this and only this can bring us to fruition
in exactly all the wrong-headed ways
this and only this will die willfully on the wind
this and only this will collect our smiles
and our songs
and our keys to unknown locks
and the lies we have chosen to believe

and our materialism
and all the things
the things!
that chain us to the lies we cannot stomach
but into which we bury our lives
this and only this
will give us the correct melody
by which to live
by which to die
by which to love
even as poorly as we are wont to do

pour whiskey down my throat
and kiss me
this is exactly the kind of task
for which my tongue was made

The Only Vow

until, until my love
that is the only vow i take with you
until, until
that time is not now
the time we are together
the time we may touch
and speak
and drink each other well
until then my love
until i can kiss you with no fear
with no brooms
waiting in the wings
with no ellipses clouding the sky
until, until my love
i will, i will
until…until…

There's Nothing Wrong with Going Soft, in Fact, It's the Hardest Thing You'll Ever Do

we men
we tired, aging men
we have never looked at our bodies with much pride
and now
as we stumble stiffly across our own thresholds
as we go soft in places
that weren't all that firm to begin with
as we recognize the damage we have done already
and still we shrug
because we men
we tired, aging men
we have never looked at our bodies
as anything other than tools
machinery
our bodies have always been the means by which we eat
the armor around our family
the mill that pumped out food and heat
the happy ending at someone else's expense

we men
we tired, forgotten shells
we argue with the days
and we shrug

To the Vincent Thomas Bridge

oh green towers
oh iron grin across the harbor
oh whore's mouth wide
sucking in all the economic effluvia of the world
oh lover so hungry for offspring of greed
oh gold digging floozy
oh classy dame sparkled in respect
we call your name, beautiful bridge
we sing your stories to the wind
men have died falling for you
and you pull us
the singers
into your horizon
and you pull us
the artists
up onto the sky, always the sky
because that is where we live
and you, oh whore
oh tired debutante
you make us see
you glow when it is dark
and make us see
you lift us up
and there, there at our fingertips
are the white mountains
there, there at our fingertips
are the cloudy saffrons of a city's collective flatulence
we are there, there
not dying
not falling for you
but we are singing your blue lighted praises
oh whore
oh favorite auntie
oh gateway to wealth
oh monument to our failures
oh dedication of indifference
oh waterlogged memorial of forgotten histories
welcome us to our doomed glory

invite us to the pointless dance
we will still sing of you
we will still tell your stories
for they are our stories
they are our foibles that cling to your railings
shimmering in the breeze
each with a morality play imprinted upon it
each with a lesson to be learned
and with each passing wave
more cling
more shimmer in the salt-laden wind
more of us fall from those shimmering railings
more of us tremble at the daylight reflected
more of us reach for the flask
and hope it is not really our story
now hanging from that rail
we reach for some measure of truth and hope
we hope that when it is our turn to fall
that we may never know it
that the water will not wake us on impact
that the shimmering is all the immortality we may reasonably reach for

oh green towers
oh shimmering icon
oh loss of integrity
oh builder of dreams
oh glory
oh greed
oh broken hearts and missing children
oh suicides
oh labor riots
oh lies we tell ourselves at night
oh bridge of commerce
oh iron link
oh scaffolding of romance and eminent domain
oh city fathers
oh captains of industry
oh dedication to greed
oh misnomer of hope and progress
oh monolith before which we all bow
of thee i sing

The Strange Pause

oh my dear one
it is the hum of us, yes?
the tired excitement
of once again
touch again
oh my dear one
it is the yes of us, no?
the always ever-after
the faraway eyes
or the soundtrack for each kiss

my dear one, yes
of this i am sure
it is the strange pause
eye to eye
it is the inedible moments
that change us, my dear one, yes
they change us

there it is again, no?
the hum of us
that generating moment hum
that momentum
the…um
it's there, isn't it dear one?
it is there for us, yes?
it is

it is
the hum of us
it is

Me to Fall

it's always your eyes
the far away of them
the laughing of them
that calls my name
that sings to my wanting
it's always
your eyes
humming so eloquently
syllables of desire
ellipses of longing
it is your eyes
calling me to fall

it is your eyes
that will catch me

Missing You Poem #1

i'm sending up flags
hoping you will see them
they are foreign flags
flags you probably won't recognize
that's how i'll know...

Missing You Poem #2

i am lonely and curious
i am aware and limping
tell me that i am not alone
i will not believe you
tell me you love my face
i will want to believe you
tell me i am the only
and i will fall
i will fall no matter what you tell me
it is my most charming fault

Missing You Poem #3

i am broken and the sky is heavy

Talkin' Lost Goddess Blues

you are still my muse
no, don't say anything
it wouldn't do either of us any good
but it's okay
i don't have to see you to taste your skin
it still tastes like poetry
i don't have to hear you
to roam your voice
to hum your breath
you are still my muse
and it is the only way i can figure out
to not completely miss you

Missing You Poem #4

he watches the rain and waits
for the phone call that will not come
he watches the rain
and wonders if his longing has an equal
in someone else's heart

A Priest Walks into a Bar…

a fan…
a fan
and the feathers there
like drunks in a confessional
like retired sommeliers making fun of the tourists

a fan…
a fan that needs a degree in electrical engineering
just to turn itself on
a fan immune to the speed gun
a fan begging to be a tree
in a dry lake bed
a fan brandishing its hat at the courtroom

a fan…
a fan and feathers
and drunk garbage men
kneading their tomorrows like a sponge salesman
desperate to save his career

a fan…
a fan and a beer
and some feathers
all sucking the confessions out
dusting his furniture with transposed begging

And I Do…

she

is beautiful
face full of sun
the night sky waiting its turn

she

a casual nymph
wrapped in the diaspora
seeking the justice of love

she

misanthropic ambassador of spontaneity
and caution
and inspiration
and insulation

she

dancing slowly along the shore
inviting the water
to come join us

she

twirling imaginary batons
set aflame with imagery
that cuts and comforts
glides and stumbles
smooth
foreign
and washing over me
pelting my skin with hard truths

she

makes me wait

and i do

Mystery is What We Hope For

it surprised me the first time i noticed
how delicate her hands were
remarkably small when held
palm to palm
against my own
fingers tendrilling against my skin
wrists turning toward the sun
a blossom she could not hold
but was

it surprised me the first time she kissed me
i was prey that day
the humidity bounced
as her delicate moved in
as her soft petal greeting launched against my mouth
acquiesce
the only word i could find

it surprised me the first time she loved me
out loud
the enunciation of starlit waves
the elucidation of horns stylizing the dim reflections
out loud it was different
out loud it had power
her mouth a blossoming burst
a flowering firework
out loud with her eyes closed
so as not to spoil the waves of sound
the waves of delicate power
the horns of blossoming power
with a vision that could not be put into words
no, better this way
better blind
and loud
out loud
it surprised me when she loved me
out loud
it surprised me how delicate it sounded

her hands dancing on my lips
my palm pressing against forever
against disappointed skies
my hands grasping for the syllables
escaping her lips
it surprised me how delicately her love
destroyed everything i needed it to
and encircled me with her out loud
with her delicate
with her blossoming burst

After the First Poem...

"you wrote about my hands"

yes...and likely will again

i will write about your skin
and your eyes
and the echoes of tomorrow they shadow
i will write about the sorrow on your brow
the wonder in your ears
i will go up river into your heart
and the darkness will hold me
illuminate me
i will photograph your fears
and develop negative stereotypes
i will document the way your courage
climbs and sings
every damned day

i will report back to the gods
that i have found something
something worth writing
something worth loving
something worth...

No Thing at All

this is why we need space…
…and time

this is how we fall flat
when flinging our hearts forward
as if there were actually such a direction

this is why we should move slow
this is why we can't
this is the viscosity of attraction
the viciousness of romance
the sharper edges of affection

this…
this is the end of no thing at all
for this forward we foolishly claim
is a curve around our own hearts
it is a boomerang collusion
between our kisses and our fears
and if there is no forward
there is only backward

backward and the nobility of failure

this…
this space that we seek
this slowing of pace in which we place our faith
it is only the self-imposed delusion of sanity
we can only pretend to not feel
we cannot not feel
it is impossible
our hearts were born to this painful gift
our eyes have seen such that they may never not see again
this is why we shy away
why we are braver than ever
why we lie mostly to our own conscience
this is how we lose ourselves
daily, yearly

this is why we are always afraid
this is why we are all so ashamed
this…
…this is the why
the how
this is that space
that time
that we so desperately need…

Nobody

nobody tells you
the stars…they're really quite cold
the light you see
is actually
literally dead…
millions of years dead…

nobody tells you
the trees…all hate you
nobody tells you the wind is never going to forgive you
nobody tells you the waves
are trying to drown you…

nobody but you…
nobody but you hammers
nobody but you weaves this wrecking ball
into my ribcage
churning bones into freedom
twisting tears into bad jokes
distilling heart-wrench into tidal basins

nobody but you, my love
knows how to wreck my head
with pain and bullshit detectors
and leave me
asking for more
your truth,
my love,
your truth…

Remember

dear one
i call to you silently

i don't want to miss you this much this soon
the room is quiet
your flutters gone
your song playing only in the echoes

dear one
i hold your name among the dog-eared pages
where it will be safe
i hold your face
still
in my beautiful trembling hands
i hold your secrets on my tongue
so that i may taste them silently
so that i may on occasion smile

dear one
your table is spare
but generous
your chairs and your creaking floor
hum loudly in the folds of my repertoire

take this, dear one
remember that i once sought
to call you by your secret name
and that i wept when you would not let me
remember that i will dream of your arm
looped through mine

remember, dear one
that i must now make this enough

She Gave Me

she gave me words
and i kissed her
she gave me metaphors
pages of resonating metaphors
all done up in fairy lights
and regret
i kissed her for the dances
for the pages of miserable love
for the resonating missives

she gave me words to which i could dance
and i forgot to ask her to join me
i will ask her…

i will ask her;
resonate with me
touch your lips to my vibrations
this is what i call a kiss
touch your palm to my missives
this is what i call dancing
touch your metaphors to my misery
this is what i call love

she gave me words
and i thanked her with my echoes

Dim Light Serenade

skin

that says yes

legs

that say…maybe

lips
that say

please

Song of the Brown-Eyed Mountain

periodically i have to remind myself
that i am in love with the sky
and that it doesn't matter that the sky is indifferent to me
it is still my sky and i share it so willingly with you
come! look at my sky!
it will blanket you with amazing and tedious
in equal measure…how can you refuse?

Sway

the things i cannot say to you
hold my ribcage prisoner
my spleen has taken a vow of silence
for the first time
ever

i will hold these words in my teeth
i will rub them smooth with my tongue
each syllable has its own distinct taste
and i will savor each one over and over
until they can sing your name on their own

the things i cannot say to you
even when i finally say them
will hold me
in their sway
as you do

in your sway

When She Trusts You Enough to Tell You That She Doesn't Trust the World

i don't want to hear those words again
i don't want to hear that sound in your voice
come
sing to me
pour it into my chest
and i will close it into a quiet chamber
so that you will know where it is
should you ever need it

And I on Mine

i would tell you that i love you
if i could
i would tell you that i miss you
if you would allow it
i would say the things to you
that burn holes in my tongue
as they are pronounced
but there is no soundtrack of strings
swelling into emotional dictates
there is no sunset into which we can fade
we are alone
you on one side of this cavernous city
and i on mine
the one that doesn't belong to me
and never will
i must court you with subversion now
it is the only way
i must find you
but only by proximity
i would say those things to you
if you would hear them
if you would miss me enough
to hear me
you see...
i fell

i fell
and i need you

Hold Nothing

in jagged notes
cascading against rainy beauty
i see your name
…
in subtle messaging
and coded dance steps
i hear your skin
seeking me
…
in dangerous markings
on the highway
i hear your tongue
beckoning
i hear your tongue
becoming
a beacon
a calling
a reason to kiss you
and the jagged notes
break on the periphery
and we are once again awash
and your name
is coding a dance
on my ribcage
your name
is cascading
against my hands
drifting through
my open fingers
…
this jagged cascade
this reason to kiss you
how can i hold them?
my hands hold nothing but desires
and your face
as i lean in once again

What I See

"look!" she said
pointing behind me
"the sun is fracturing on the edge of the world!"

"i know" i murmured
my gaze unwavering
"i've been watching it in your eyes…"

The Confession

"i trust you" she said

she said it twice
that day

she said it looking into his eyes
she said it holding firmly
onto his hand

she said it twice that day

he knew

what she really meant

Holding My Breath

your body is a flame
and i am every devotion you deserved
and never got
your emanations keep the darkness
from my nights
i have visited you in secret
i have held you in my sleep
this curve
that softness
the electric insanity
that balms my nervous system
and bombs my heart
your body is a flame
that calls to my eyes
that sings of unknown things
and starry missions
that plays against the colors
but owns only the sky
your body takes me home
and i am warm once again
your body is the moon
and i am curled against the clouds
your body is a tree
holding my breath in your boughs
your body falls into ripples of need and fascination
burn me
i am your fuel
reach into the air and claim it
your beauty is dancing on the wind
climb and climb and steal the sunset
drape it across your belly
i will watch with amazing in my eyes
your body is a flame
and i am every devotion you deserved
and never got

Cause and Effect

maybe it was the jazz filling the room
the horns invoking the night
the night invoking our heated breath
our lungs invoking our longing
our longing calling to the waves
the waves driving the night sky into swirls
the swirls dizzying the bed sheets
the bed sheets draping us in invisible glitter
the glitter grabbing and dazzling the breeze
the breeze humming hungrily in our ears
our ears tired only of the silence of want
our want dancing to the jazz filling our room
our room shrinking to become our world

Casa de la Bates

the night is naked
and the waves count us
the seagulls await the dawn

the air is cool on my skin
the ambient night glows on yours
i am in love with your hips
with the gentle but firm upslope
there on your side in silence
the sheet draping you in classicism

tonight
we are naked against the stars
we are placing ourselves
at our own mercy
tonight
as the waves count us
as the dawn awaits us
as the air envelopes our fever
tonight
with the firm but gentle upslope
of your lips
against my skin
of my tongue tasting your secret
tonight
i am in love with your hips
with your neck
with those eyes
and with the mouth
where my name lives on your tongue
warm and safe

tonight, take me
i am warm against the sky that is your belly
i am safe against the tide that is your heart
i am laughing against the songs that are your eyes
tonight, take me
i am naked against the night
and i am yours

Correction

i am the sand at your feet

no...

you are the ocean

Goddess of Here and Now

all of my lovers
have cursed me with the memory of their affections
fingerprints across my skin
drops of sweetness and pain freckle me
i see them in the night
i feel them in moments of rapture and regret

all of them...

but she...
perhaps because it is once again new
perhaps i am seeking things
i do not need to find
but she...

she is the sidewalk crack i trip on every morning
she is the raised hairs
that don't quite disturb
don't quite comfort
she is the cloud that arrests my eye
she is that moment at the red light

all of my lovers
have cursed me
(oh how some have cursed me)
but she

she wins my now
she wins my here
if only
she would come claim her laurels

Horizon

you are not the end of the night
but you are there
glistening
and if the stars have set your skin on fire
the morning blue cools you
pulling you to her breast

you are not the end of the night
but you are there
singing
echoing the canyons above us
a wing
across the arroyo

you are not the end of the night
and i sing your crazy hair
onto the breeze
i welcome the weather
through your open window
ushered by the cat
ushered by that touch
the casual one
as you roll out of bed

you are not the end of the night
but it is your blood
that warms me
when i am there

In the Empty-Walled Room

lying back
in a smoky lazy haze
his head only in the Soft Boys song
rolling out of the small speakers near the mattress
his head only listening
to the rhythms of his random thinking
filling the empty-walled room
lying back into the rhythm of his random
his head only on her heart
only on her words
the ones she said today on the phone
lying back in a smoky haze of her words
his rhythm only listening to her voice
only to the rhythm of the clouds rolling
over the mountains to the west
his head only listening
to the rhythm of her words
only to her heart in the smoky haze of her words
listening
finally
to her heart
hearing only the random words
only the smoky rhythm of her love
lying back in the haze
rolling out of the small speakers near the mattress
he weeps
staring at the ceiling
and seeing only the smoky rhythm of her love
he weeps
finally finding a rhythm with his own breathing
weeping and staring and filling the empty-walled room
his random real
his favorite rhythm
his smoky hazy mountains
buried in the sound of her voice
he weeps
knowing finally
the rhythm of his own breathing…

…(yes)…

In Which the Geographer Finds His Compass Once Again
for Armine

i am alone with you
inside the smallest chamber of my heart
it is warm
and disconcerting
the dogs run wild and happy
we dance to the rhythm of the waves
colliding down the sand
pulling down our expectations
severing our understanding
serializing our lost and silent moments

i am alone with you
on the edge of the world
and we watch it end
in what was once described as fire
we watch it end
in what was once described as ice
we watch it end
in what was once described as forever

that is when we kiss
for the first and last time
the rest of our strange waltz
falls somewhere in the middle
the rest of our broken days
sit quietly on the outskirts
waiting their turns

the condor drifting along the cliff
is curious about my dancing
the waves call your name
welcoming you back
all of us
here
alone with you
in the smallest chamber of my heart
welcome you

our dancing is the silence
that tells you
our silence is the metaphor
for what we cannot say
our metaphors are familiar and subversive
and teach us how to move
how to breathe
for respiration is simply an imitation
a substitution
a Potemkin proposition
when we breathe
we are defying the skies to claim us
our lungs are a kinetic middle finger
aimed at the inevitable

this, my love
this is why we dance
here
on the wet sand
here
in the wind
here
below the wings of retired angels
this is why we sing against the inevitable
so that here
inside the smallest chamber of my heart
the reverberations will warm us
the wings will comfort us
the skies will hold us close
here where i have saved a place for you
here where my secrets long to brush your skin
here where i have stolen all the second hands
here behind the phalanx of absurd

here
this is where i will make you a part of my geography
i will build a relief map of your body
clouds will decorate your hairline
sailboats will dock along your coastline
and as you become my landscape
i will be your first-aid kit

i will be the small scruffy dog
i will be running to tie your shoes

so when the gods come to question us
and demand that we justify our blood
we will stand naked against forever
i, to your right
you, inoculating the wind
our forefingers touch
our sweat mingles
the gods will acquiesce
and i will wake
with your head on my chest
with your skin an aurora
and i will know where i am

Tonight I Will

tonight i will place
a rock in your garden
at the base of your roses
there
by your front door
tonight i will place
a rock that came to me
from ancient peru
brought to me by a man

tonight
in secret
i will give to you a rock
and my ancient love
will complete an unknown spell
my words will be random
as usual
and you will feel things
you cannot name
i promise you
there is no need
instead
let these things name you
let these things caress your neck
and call to you in the night
tonight i will place
a rock in your garden
my name in your ribcage
my lips upon your skin

Will

your skin sings
your skin is on fire

i kiss it gently
searching for truth
i find mythology worthy of the ages
i find instruments of the sweetest torture
i find echoes of the world
in your skin

i kiss it gently
and i am inflamed
i burn from every misstep in my life
i burn from the brokenness
i have left in my stumbling wake
i burn for the song i hear
on your skin
in those eyes
from your lips
as they sear my longing

your skin sings
your skin is on fire

i will kiss it gently
you will
engulf me

This is Where

dear one
when i place my head on your belly
it is because i am in need
when i stare at you while you sleep
it is because i am afraid i will miss something

dear one
my life is a sunshine massacre
and yet you turn here
picking up broken mirrors
picking up useful bits of sorrow
knitting my brows into something apocryphal

dear one
tell me a story
sing to me of genocide and lavender
acquire the rights to the legend of your shadow
tell the border guards that they are loved
no one else knows how
and they have waited so long

dear one
when i place my head on your belly
it is because this is where
this is where the world gets lost
this is where the wind finds itself
and stops searching
this is where minor characters get their due
this is where we frisk ourselves
looking for a match and find a loosened fist instead

dear one
call to me when it is cold
i will come
call to me when the sky is vile
i will come
call to me when the beast dances brutally on your bad knee
i will come

dear one
call to me
you know already
all of the names i may use
call to me
my ribcage will answer
my calluses will answer
my intentions will answer
my epiphanies will answer
call to me dear one
and my soliloquies will resolve
my subtext will be written in neon
call to me dear one

i will hear you

The Crown

next time
i will embrace you in the water
and we will let the waves fall over us...

just as we do
on land...

next time
i will make your name into a kite
and hang it high above the cliff top...

so that everyone can learn to spell...

next time
i will hold the moon to your cheek
as we watch the sun fall away...

your eyes reflecting every moment of glow
every teardrop of curiosity...

next time
i will move the world to your doorstep
and the sky will finally relent
our entreaties will be heard...

...next time,
the crown will be the next time

The Song I Will Sing to You

the song i will sing to you
is hidden
in the echoes that linger
among the darkness you call hair

i am looking
listening

the melody is the color of your eyes
the chorus is somewhere on your skin
i will place my ear against your breast
to count your heartbeats
so that i will know the meter of the song i will sing to you

the song i will sing to you
is about loss and night skies
it is about falling and smiling
this song is afraid and full of dance

the song i will sing to you
is buried in my lungs
and reaching for the sky
it is raising the hairs on my neck
the song is my turn signal
it is the scent of fresh garlic
it is me stumbling through the alley
whiskey on my breath

the song i will sing to you
knows loneliness is only a teacher
understands that we are all on fire
the song i will sing to you
is a broken roadmap that will never lose you

the song i will sing to you
is composed of those moments
when you catch me staring into your eyes
the gentle brush of the cheek

your arm linked through mine
the song jumps from one to the other
it moves the air across our skin
the song kisses us in the gentlest of places
it bruises us in the most beautiful of ways

the song i will sing to you

i'm looking for it
i'm listening to your heartbeat
"tapping out rhythms
tapping out rhythms"
i'm kissing your skin
calling the song to rise from your pores
so that i can inhale
and breathe out the melody that is you

And in Silence

the gentle movement of her hands
the tiny knuckles
the brushed intimations of her fingertips

the purposeful flow and flutter
as she calls down her heritage
taps into the skein of hospitality
as she undresses her body
as she undresses my body
as she pulls me
claims me
calls me

the soft power of her grip
the sliding scale of ownership
the mouthful of optimism
the circulating touch of shackles being lost

the split infinitive of lost and broken
the lyric content of suicide notes

the articulating dance across my belly
the sharpened greeting with every warm push-me-pull-you
her hands so strong
her voice so exponential
the surprising delicacies
of these star-hungry extensions
they are seekers
and questioners
each finger a curved query
a hint of imagination

the gentle, tiny, brushed intimidations
grip me in silence
and in silence
i dance

At Times

yes love, yes
you are sensitive
yes love, yes
you *feel*
at times exquisitely
at times brutally

yes love, yes
i see you
and it is not your fault
it is not a fault at all
it is that you see what others don't
you see what others won't
at times exquisitely
at times brutally

yes love, yes
i see you
and i know
at times exquisitely...

Of Keeping Pace

the beautiful task
of walking
arm in arm with her
feeling the slight pressure
in the crook of my elbow
shoulders bumping lightly
every few strides
glancing left and seeing
that smile
those eyes
turned up into my face
the waves of amazing
that fall over me
and the warm aliving of my skin
the special errand
of keeping pace
with beauty
with the crenellated enticements
shimmering
dancing
teasing
the formidable exercise
of remembering carefully
every
single
step

Know This

you may not know this
at night sometimes
i wake
i sit
and i watch you
i watch your body
after midnight
i watch your breathing
in the moonlight
i watch your skin
reflecting the stars
i watch you stretch each limb
in turn
listening in the darkness
to the springs moaning beneath you
i watch you
after midnight
and you may not know this
but this is how i fell

after midnight
i was claimed
in the moonlight
my ribcage extended itself
in the starlight
your skin came to me and sang
you may not know this

this is how i fell

How

remember that day?
the one where the mountains darkened
and the sky held on for dear light?
when we swam into each other?
when we got drunk on the sky?
when Tuscany was our dream?

remember that day?
the day we sat on the bed
reading Sexton to each other?
remember how we would laugh
at all the wrong places?

remember that day?
how we howled at the stars?
how we found ourselves entangled and immune?
remember how we danced on the dream beach?
remember the animal sounds?
and the oak trees?
remember the branches growing into each other?
reaching up like a giant hand
into the sky?
remember how we climbed that tree together
in our collective dream?
remember the tree house we built
resting on multiple branches?

remember that day?
remember the overcast dawn?
remember how i loved you?

You in the Dark

…sweet silence and soft auburn hair…

— Townes Van Zandt

you should stop sometimes
and see the lights
yes, it is dark
yes, it is all looming
but, oh, if you listen
the waves will sing your name
and the night will love you
you should stop sometimes

oh, but you do, my love
you stop and turn in the night
and tell me with an accidental touch
oh, but you do, my love
you tell me in the silence
your breath following your curves in the night
as my eyes
as my dreams

i stop sometimes
in the night
and see the lights of your skin
of your hair in the shadows
of your imminence

my love
this is you
on a wing
this is you
when i am almost the loneliest i have ever been
my love
this is you
on my mind
fluttering against my bones
calling from the deep
this is you
when i see you in the dark

understand,
even now i look at you in the night
even now i am mystified
even now i shake, ever so briefly
with the flash of fear

even now, my love, i stop sometimes
i stop and look at you
as if you just might disappear
as if i did not just stir in the night
as if this were still my dream

even now, my love
i stop
to look at your light

About the Author

As poetry rarely pays well, David McIntire has taken on numerous occupations over the years including printer, flooring installer, private investigator, delivery boy, factotum, retail manager, warehouse worker, pharmacy technician, Uber driver and roadie. His poetry has been translated into Swedish of all things. David lives in Portland. His books, *Punk Rock Breakfast* and *No One Will Believe You: Songs of the Aftermath*, are published by Baxter Daniels Ink Press/International Word Bank.

FREE MUMIA
FREE PELTIER

Acknowledgments

without whom, etc.....Armine Iknadossian, Marina and Elliot McIntire, Red O'Hare, Eric Morago, Brenda Petrakos, Murray Thomas, Richard Modiano, S.A. Griffin, Brian & Callie and the whole Eastburn crew, 2-bit Whore...

...and as ever Scott Wannberg

cover art *A Salute from the Underground* hand drawn by M. Segal (from his photograph) with color by 11:21

Other books by David McIntire

No One Will Believe You
Punk Rock Breakfast

chapbooks

Exit Wounds
Other
Beat Up the Poor
Love, Death, Etc.

Patrons

Moon Tide Press would like to thank the following people for their support in helping publish the finest poetry from the Southern California region. To sign up as a patron, visit www.moontidepress. com or send an email to publisher@moontidepress.com.

Anonymous
Robin Axworthy
Conner Brenner
Bill Cushing
Susan Davis
Peggy Dobreer
Dennis Gowans
Half Off Books & Brad T. Cox
Jim & Vicky Hoggatt
Ron Koertge & Bianca Richards
Ray & Christi Lacoste
Zachary & Tammy Locklin
Lincoln McElwee
David McIntire
José Enrique Medina
Andrew November
Michael Miller & Rachanee Srisavasdi
Terri Niccum
Ronny & Richard Morago
Jennifer Smith
Andrew Turner
Mariano Zaro

Also Available from Moon Tide Press

Letters to the Leader, HanaLena Fennel (2019)
Darwin's Garden, Lee Rossi (2019)
Dark Ink: A Poetry Anthology Inspired by Horror (2018)
Drop and Dazzle, Peggy Dobreer (2018)
Junkie Wife, Alexis Rhone Fancher (2018)
The Moon, My Lover, My Mother, & the Dog, Daniel McGinn (2018)
Lullaby of Teeth: An Anthology of Southern California Poetry (2017)
Angels in Seven, Michael Miller (2016)
A Likely Story, Robbi Nester (2014)
Embers on the Stairs, Ruth Bavetta (2014)
The Green of Sunset, John Brantingham (2013)
The Savagery of Bone, Timothy Matthew Perez (2013)
The Silence of Doorways, Sharon Venezio (2013)
Cosmos: An Anthology of Southern California Poetry (2012)
Straws and Shadows, Irena Praitis (2012)
In the Lake of Your Bones, Peggy Dobreer (2012)
I Was Building Up to Something, Susan Davis (2011)
Hopeless Cases, Michael Kramer (2011)
One World, Gail Newman (2011)
What We Ache For, Eric Morago (2010)
Now and Then, Lee Mallory (2009)
Pop Art: An Anthology of Southern California Poetry (2009)
In the Heaven of Never Before, Carine Topal (2008)
A Wild Region, Kate Buckley (2008)
Carving in Bone: An Anthology of Orange County Poetry (2007)
Kindness from a Dark God, Ben Trigg (2007)
A Thin Strand of Lights, Ricki Mandeville (2006)
Sleepyhead Assassins, Mindy Nettifee (2006)
Tide Pools: An Anthology of Orange County Poetry (2006)
Lost American Nights: Lyrics & Poems, Michael Ubaldini (2006)

www.ingramcontent.com/pod-product-compliance
Lightning Source LLC
Chambersburg PA
CBHW020919090426
42736CB00008B/709